TITCHFIELD:
A Century of Change

FROM OLD PHOTOGRAPHS

compiled by
Titchfield History Society

TITCHFIELD: A CENTURY OF CHANGE
FROM OLD PHOTOGRAPHS

Published by Titchfield History Society 2019
ISBN 978-0-903421-30-3

Titchfield History Society

www.titchfieldhistorysociety.com

A catalogue description of this book is available from the British Library

Contents

Acknowledgements

The following have collaborated to produce this publication

Phil Burner - Contemporary Photographs
Bryan Dunleavy – Book Design
Amanda Laws – Text
Peter Noyce – Images
Colin & Marilyn Wilton-Smith – Text

THS

Introduction

Walking along many streets in Titchfield it is easy to imagine what it must have been like 100 years ago and, even in some parts, back several centuries. It is only when looking at the old images that we discover just how many small, yet important elements of our townscape are different. The change from gas lighting to electric, the slow increase in traffic signs, parked cars instead of pedestrians and the reduction of retail premises in favour of homes.

One itinerant photographer came to the village in about 1906. Accompanying those images one can almost hear the cry of excitement from groups of children running down West Street and coming along East Street, as the 'Titchfield grapevine' tells them that a man with a big black box is taking a 'likeness' of the village.

The subtle alteration of shop windows and wholesale demolishing of cottages was then seen as a sign of progress. The damming of the tidal estuary to Titchfield in the 17th century and the bypass in the 20th both caused economic hardship to local workers at the time, yet now are just part of the history of the village. As this is being written the clock, put up in the village in 1988 to celebrate the best kept village award, has been resited on the butchers in South Street.

Several streets in Titchfield include houses owned by the Earl of Southampton Trust, a merging of several bequests dating from the 16th century this support given to others for me epitomises the history of the people of Titchfield.

Within The Titchfield History Society there is always someone who is planning and researching towards a publication. Often these can take years to come to fruition, while facts are being found and double checked. Some people have spent a lifetime searching for old images of Titchfield in dusty second hand bookshops and antique fairs and more recently using the internet. Some images still elude us, the view from the mill towards the village before the bypass and the cottages on Church Path.

This book is a culmination of the diligent foraging of residents and historians and for these efforts the History Society are very grateful.

MILL LANE - Titchfield Tithe Barn built after 1407.

Along Mill Lane

Before the toll road was built in 1810 the unmade road called Mill Street (previously known as North Street) was the main route out of Titchfield going north and east. It passed the Mill and the Abbey and those on horseback, cart or foot could turn right over the Anjou (Stony) Bridge, up Fishers Hill to Catisfield or straight on to Funtley. Those wishing to travel to Portsmouth or Southampton often used the easier sea route, as dirt tracks were impassable in bad weather.

Mill Street was home to the workhouse from 1732 to the 1830's. In 1902 land was donated to the village to build the Drill Hall for local army volunteer servicemen, this is where the Community Centre now stands. In 1932 nine cottages were demolished at the end of Mill Street to make way for the building of the Titchfield Bypass, completed in October 1933.

FISHERS HILL - This shows the original route to Fareham and beyond across the Stony/Anjou Bridge. The view of the fields behind is obscured now by trees, without the road markings and foliage the view would be identical.
Left: The Stony/Anjou Bridge today. No views and the road has been slightly built up leaving the height of the walls slightly lower.

THE ABBEY/PLACE HOUSE - Looking west down towards the abbey from Fishers Hill showing the Railway Inn, now the Fishermans Rest, in the foreground. The cottage attached to the inn was a separate dwelling
Left: The same view taken slightly to the south to capture the abbey, although Fishermans Rest obscured by trees.

THE ABBEY/PLACE HOUSE – Completely unkept with trees and foliage growing out of the stonework and chimneys.
Left: A clean looking abbey having been restored in the 1980s

FISHERMANS

MILL LANE - The Fishermans Rest around the 1950s is still visible from across the river.
Left: The Fisherman's Rest today taken from the end of the garden as trees now obscure it from view.

THE MILL - The changing face and usage of the mill over the years, the trolleys on this day lined up outside.
Right: It was once located in Mill Street, but due to the construction of the A27 in 1933, it is now part of Mill Lane and is a pub of the same name. Apart from the large canopy it remains largely unchanged.

SPECIAL OFFERS

MILL STREET - Looking north along the street, the projecting cottage towards the end is advertising 'Thomas Bennett Shoe and Boot Makers'. The property on the left hand corner was originally 'The Crown' until it lost its licence in 1906.

e Wheatsheaf
this car park is for
ATRONS ONLY
VN60 NUV

MILL STREET - An image from further down the street towards the mill. The stables to the rear of 'The Wheatsheaf' on the left are now the parking area and gardens for pub and the house on the right has a garage entrance.

MILL STREET - 'Willowbank' on the right, once the home of the Parr family, has been altered with the stucco and external shutters removed, together with the Georgian railings. A horse and trap waits outside.

EAST STREET - The Regent Oil Company existed from 1947 to 1956 when they were taken over by Texaco. The Automobile Association sign is above the original garage premises. On the left hand side, one of the few sets of original Georgian railings are visible.

East Street

Once busy with pubs at both ends of the street, chocolate shops, private schools in front parlours and in the 1960's the Lyons Maid ice cream premises, East Street is now primarily small terrace cottages, originally homes for those working at the brewery or tannery or with other skilled trades such as carpenters or bricklayers.

Larger properties built in the Georgian period dominate the eastern end where the toll road was pushed through, much to the consternation of Captain Thompson who lost his meadow. The pathway in the northwest corner to the new school was called The Harris, a name now lost in the mists of time. East Street featured in the film 'Landfall' about an RAF Pilot in WWII.

P
Long stay
Community centre

EAST STREET - 'Upshalls' Service Garage established in the 1924 and closing its doors in 2018.
Left: Three new properties recently built on the site.

EAST STREET - The street is now dominated by parked cars and the shops converted back into residential properties. Sheep are probably being driven back from Fareham Market, as at this time Titchfield's Market didn't exist.

EAST STREET - View of the old shop fronts along the north side of the road and a glimpse of number 28 being used as a café.
Left: All the shop fronts converted to residential properties.

LAND ROVER
BN55 JZO

EAST STREET – An early view of The Wheatsheaf showing that it once had stables and accommodation for cyclists. The adjoining cottage advertising 'Nugget's Shoe Polish'.
Left: The Wheatsheaf now has an updated frontage but the terrace remains virtually the same.

EAST STREET - Right: West end of the street, a thriving dressmaking business and George Barfoot's Gentleman's Outfitters. A gentleman's horse and trap awaits outside probably whilst he is having a suit measured.
Above: No more shops but frontages sympathetically converted.

G. BARFOOT. DRAPER & OUTFITTER.
GH CLASS
ESSMAKING.

SOUTHAMPTON HILL - The villas on Southampton Hill were newly built on the cusp of the Edwardian era. By the time this picture was taken in the 1920's Titchfield had just got electric lighting, mains water and sewage. Only the unmade road and a gap in the row of houses distinguishes it from the present day view.

Southampton Hill

As the name suggests Southampton Hill is another early route out of the village. Until the 1890's other than a small cottage at the top, to the south were fields and to the north was part of the garden for what is now known as the Old Lodge. The Parish Room was added in 1891 and the villas on the south side were first built on the fields in around 1900. By the 1920's petrol and repair garages had opened on both sides and after a spate of car accidents at the bottom of the hill, two cottages were demolished in 1924 to improve the junction. In 1945 a number of council funded houses were built on land belonging to Old Lodge and in 1954 another ten were added. The new fire station opened on Southampton Hill in July 1952, now redeveloped into homes.

SOUTHAMPTON HILL - Looking east down Southampton Hill before the development on the left hand side.
Left: the development of early 20th century housing can clearly be seen, with the road having been widened for parking purposes.

SOUTHAMPTON HILL

SOUTHAMPTON HILL - Looking west up the hill showing the two opposing garages. 'BP' and 'Esso'. The road at that time was a main road out of the village.
Left: New development on both sides where the garages once stood. The left hand was first built as offices but these buildings are now residential.

THE SQUARE -In the 1950's a gas showroom is situated next to the Bugle where the Co-op is today. Inset: The Market Hall which once stood in the Square.

High Street and The Square

Titchfield's early medieval street plan is most obvious in our existing central square, used for holding a market from the 11th century. Despite the redesigned fronts of many early timber framed houses in this street the view has changed little over centuries.

The Market Hall, gifted to the village by the Earl of Southampton in 1619, was an attempt to resurrect Titchfield's market after the closing of the estuary caused an economic slump. It was moved out of the Square about 1810 and now takes pride of place at The Weald and Downland Living Museum.

The High Street was also home to an alternative religious meeting house as early as the mid 17th century, which became The Independent chapel in 1789. The building was updated the following century and now called the Evangelical Church.

P
WC
Short Stay
Jubilee Surgery
SOUTHAMPTO

HIGH STREET - Looking along the High Street towards the Square the new road signs and cars are the only obvious changes to this view from the 1950's.
Subtle alterations to the buildings include Victorian bay windows on what is now the Chinese Takeaway and 8 & 8A was a single house with one front door.

WILLIAM HUDSON
OLD FREE
HOUSE

Hill & Bond
BARBERS OF TITCHFIELD
Hays Travel
The co-operative Titchfield

THE SQUARE - Present day views of the Square illustrated on the previous and following pages. The motor car has made a big impact!

OLD FREE
HOUSE

NESTLE'S
MILK
STEAM BAKERY
TRINITY ROAD
HOVIS
BREAD

Hill & Bond
Find the home you deserve
BARBERS OF TITCHFIELD
Hays Travel
QUIKSILVER

THE SQUARE - The village decked out to celebrate George V's jubilee in 1935. Lancaster and Crook grocery and hardware in the foreground with the number 45A bus on its way to Southampton. A lovely old charabanc from company called 'The Don'.

P Community Centre (Long stay)
P Short stay

THE SQUARE - The north corner of the square has hardly changed. The village dressed with banners and crowns for the Coronation of Queen Elizabeth II in 1953 .

THE HIGH STREET - Looking north showing the cottages that once stood on the corner of Southampton Hill. Maybury's covered in ivy. Busy looking shop premises.
Above: The properties which once stood on the corner were demolished to make way for road widening. The Earl of Southampton Trust cottages and the 'Queen's Head" on the west side are largely unchanged.

JADE PALACE
WL61 PXT

THE HIGH STREET - Harry Childs on a horse drawn cab outside Titchfield Post Office around 1912 situated opposite the Queen's Head at this time.
The cottages that were once the post office have reverted to residential use.

CHURCH STREET – By the 1950's Bungey's had become a toy shop and A J Hales the bicycle shop was opposite, both clear in the memories of our older residents.

Church Street

From existing photographs once past Mr Bungey's premises the street appears to have been almost entirely residential, although number 11 has an early shop window on the front, possibly a Victorian boot maker. Most residents identified on the census returns from the time these early photographs were taken were market gardeners and agricultural labourers. Major changes to the Church had already taken place in the mid Victorian period, although it has been extended more recently to the south, Other than a new weathervane in 1914 little seems to have altered when looking at the images of the church. The rectory was replaced in 1852 after a fire and the churchyard was also expanded towards the canal. This was finally replaced as the main burial ground for Titchfield around 1918 when the cemetery on Posbrooke Lane was established.

CHURCH STREET – 'Bungay's Saddlers' on the corner of the Square and Church Street looking toward the Church. The shop on the right was vacant at the time.
Above: Bungay's original shop front having had the Georgian frontage removed and chimneys straightened.

H. BUNGEY
SADDLER &
Harness Maker

MEON BRIDGE - A metal bridge around the 1930s, crossing the canal from the churchyard, a very open view across to the Tannery in the distance.
Left: A replacement wooden bridge taken from a slightly different angle, as original photograph position is now unreachable.

REST

ST PETER'S CHURCHYARD - A very unkept churchyard taken before 1909. The railings around the box tombs were probably later removed for the war effort. The grave on the right in the foreground is for the Heath family from South Street.
Left: A much clearer looking scene, the Chapter Rooms having been added to the side of the church.

ST PETER'S CHURCH - Right: the Church seen from the vicarage garden in 1905 a very tidy looking churchyard with the railings around the box tombs.
From the same position very little can be seen of the church due to the high hedge grown around the garden of the now 'old vicarage' property which is now a private residence

The weather is very cold here now
Oct 5th 05

WEST STREET – The National School at the top of West Street was built in 1830 and enlarged in subsequent years as Titchfield's population grew. At the time of this photograph about 350 pupils were on roll and it was superseded in 1933 by the present school on the bypass.

West Street

The abundance of small workers cottages lining the street were built up particularly on the north side before 1850. Like other streets, West Street was dominated by market gardeners and agricultural workers and was the route out to the fields of Titchfield Common and the Meon.

Possibly our earliest Coaching Inn (serving by 1546), was the West End Inn, both old and new versions having now been converted into houses. The first National School in the village was built in 1830 up the hill and many of our young Titchfield WWI recruits were past pupils of the school.

A number of cottages were pulled down in 1937; part way up the street and on the corner of South Street, an overzealous public health inspector deemed them unfit for human habitation.

No 61
Anjou
Cottage

WEST STREET – At the top of West Street with the church spire in the distance, without the cars this would be a very unchanged view. Lots of people going about their daily business on a warm day, windows open, some work was going on outside number 63-69 and the timber framed cottages can be seen at the bottom of the street.

WEST STREET - A 16th century timber framed building as two or possibly three cottages at the time. Well-worn steps leading to front doors. Left: The property was fully restored in the 20th century. Note the Emblem flag flying.

PEUGEOT
207 SW
7

WEST STREET – Looking up the street showing the new 'West End Inn' on the left.
Above: An earlier photograph looking up the street showing the 'West End Inn', built in 1912.

30
30

WEST STREET – An early photograph looking up the street showing the original 'West End Inn', and the thatched cottages where the new pub was built.

WEST END
INN
GXZ
4248

WEST STREET – Further along the street showing cottages opposite the 'West End Inn'. The first cottage on the right was for some time 'Caroline Bungey's Sweet Shop'.
Left: The street is now entirely residential.

ND12 NYN

WEST STREET – Taken from the Square the properties on the right were originally store houses, and cottages stood on the left in the foreground until the 1930s.
Left: The land in the foreground is now the village green and the old store houses have been adapted for other uses.

South Street

This street was home to some of Titchfield's oldest families, names such as Frampton and Bedford can be found on census returns when these early images were taken. There was a mixture of agricultural workers, market gardeners and small businesses at the turn of the last century and at least two pubs. Dominated by the timber framed cottages, at first glance it seems to be the street which has least changed. In fact there have been several houses demolished from the 1930's to 1960's at both ends of the street and in the middle. The original Coach and Horses was rebuilt in 1926 and more recently demolished for housing. It was only the outcry from the Titchfield residents that saved the street as it is today, when the local council proposed wholesale demolition to widen the road in 1939.

SOUTH STREET – Right: Showing 'Oily Williams' premises and delivery business incorporating the 'Tin Tabernacle' building. An original general store with many metal advertising signs adorning the walls.

NESTLÉ'S MILK
"The Richest in Cream"
PRATT'S SPIRIT
LONGSTERS
SEWING MACHINES REPAIRED
G.L. WILLIAMS.
OIL MERCHANT.
CHOCOLATE
NESTLES MILK
LYONS TEA
NECTAR TEA
OIL

PLE
KS

SOUTH STREET – Looking north showing the 'Red House' as the location for the Post Office at that time, an early shop front to the left of the picture.
Left: The 'Red House' is now residential and the original old shop front opposite has been replaced by two modern town houses.

SOUTH STREET – Looking north toward The Square, a bustling scene with 'The King's Head' pub on the right and many shop fronts and trades along the street.
'The King's Head' now a residential property named 'Cordwainers'.

FOR SALE

SOUTH STREET – The jettied houses, which are original medieval timber framed properties and looking fairly fragile at this date. The jettied houses today having been fully restored with the end cottage being incorporated. The properties are flagged and flowered ready for 'Britain in Bloom' judging day

SOUTH STREET – Looking south towards the junction of Bridge Street and Coach Hill. Traffic calming measures, a consequence of increasing number of vehicles along the narrow road, now characterise South Street.
This view shows a dilapidated state of the early 15th century jettied houses and on the right most of this row have now been replaced.

Taylor Hill & Bond
FOR SALE
0800 292 2825

SOUTH STREET – These houses have needed intermittent repair for nearly 600 years, although now Health and Safety would now suggest scaffolding rather than this makeshift arrangement of tables.

30
30

SOUTH STREET – Top of the street at the junction with Builder and Undertaker 'T Conway' on the left, and the road in front of it at the time named 'Castle Street'.
Left: The corner property still run as a Funeral Directors 'Freemantle's'. The road in front now known as 'Frog Lane'. The road widened for parking area but narrowed at the junction for traffic control.

SOUTH STREET – The small roundabout slows the traffic where South Street meets Bridge Street and Coach Hill. Not always slow enough, as can be seen by a bay window recently damaged by a car.
The Old Surgery and Fielders Brewery are in the background of this image and the undertakers on the left. The children continued to follow the photographer and a man in an apron stopped work for the picture.

30
Zone ENDS

COACH HILL JUNCTION – The original "Coach and Horses' public house, which had a theatre attached, was replaced by a newer building in 1926. (See page 100) Left: New properties sympathetically built incorporating parts of the original pub and theatre now stand on the site.

20
ZONE
ZONE
BRIDGE STREET

SOUTH STREET – Looking down the street from Coach Hill, the cottage facing has a Barber's pole outside. Showing the modern properties built on the vacant land to the left. Barber's shop premises no longer exists.

SOUTH STREET – The New Coach and Horses served the village for 80 years before the site was redeveloped.

Coach Hill and Bridge Street

Two obvious routes in and out of this once busy market town, Bridge Street, requiring a crossing at the canal, has been dominated by Fielders Brewery buildings since 1744 and included the Brewery Tavern and opposite a pub called 'The George'. William Doe, a coal merchant traded on the street and later the Titchfield & District Lighting Co Ltd (Gas works).

Coach Hill, in the past was called Coach Lane and featured smart houses for Captains retired from the Navy. It took until the 20th century for either street to have other properties on the south side, where before was open countryside and managed fields.

BRIDGE STREET

BRIDGE STREET - On the junction looking east 'Fielders Brewery' on the right. The 'Old Surgery' was completely covered in ivy.
Left: Part of the brewery having been demolished and now a cleaner looking house on the corner. Note the chimneys have hardly altered.

COACH HILL – A view taken between the wars looking towards the junction of South Street. Note all the different sized ladders up against number 3.
Left: This could almost be the same photograph with only a few recent updates.

BRIDGE STREET - Fielder's Brewery in Bridge Street. The style of the car giving away the date of 1960s.
Left: Very little remains of the original brewery. The remaining building is now a residential property

STREET

BRIDGE STREET – Lovely rural scene from the Bridge at the turn of the 20th Century
Left: A very different scene, the canal obscured by vegetation.

BRIDGE STREET – Looking west a delivery lorry turning out the 'Fielder's Brewery' at the end of the road.
Left: This modern view shows that time has done little to alter the line of the properties.

BRIDGE STREET – View looking East towards Hollam farm prior to the Stubbington Road being constructed.
Left: Trees and overgrown hedges from uncultivated fields block the original view.

We hope, through this book, you enjoy walking along the streets and lanes of Titchfield.

BV - #0200 - 170523 - C0 - 152/229/7 - PB - 9780993421303 - Gloss Lamination